GROWING UP WI1

by

J. Smith Kirkland

copyright 2016

Dedicated to

people who have given me

wonderful memories of growing up:

My Sisters

My Parents

My Grandmothers

And my Aunt Mae

Searching skywards for a sign

a truth, a way, a light, a word

searching skywords

About This Collection

Before there was the internet, and cable television, and video games, I was learning about the world by watching the world around me. The observations I made became memories, which became stories that replay in my head. Sometimes, the stories came out later as poetry. And sometimes, I would see things around me that somehow reminded me of one of the stories, and I would try to capture it in a photograph. This book is a collection of my stories as essays, and poetry, and pictures.

There are stories that I tell frequently, and memories that I only share on rare occasion. Some people have heard some of the stories perhaps too many times, and some memories have not been heard by anyone at all. These stories and memories, these little fragments of my life, have held onto their place in my brain for years, even decades. They have wired themselves to thousands of synapses so that they can't be lost, and the oddest words or moments trigger them to be replayed in my mind. I may forget the name of the people who live down the hall, or the PIN for my credit card, or sometimes even my own telephone number, but these moments are as clear to me now as if they had just happened.

These pages are my attempt to record the stories and memories that are deeply embedded into my essence. There is no intent to educate, philosophy, or even amuse. For now, this is a mere exercise in making notes. A collection of fragments of moments I remember. If there is a moral to the stories, or some explanation in them for why I sometimes feel 40 degrees to the left of the rest of the world, well, perhaps I will see it when I am done. Maybe you will see it before me.

40 Degrees to the Left

When I was in first grade, we were learning to write. We began by drawing straight vertical lines on our first grade ruled paper, the kind with two solid lines for the top and bottom of capital letters, and a dashed line in the center, so we could make lower case letters with uniform heights. The teacher came by and turned my paper so that it was straight with the table's edge. She said, "no wonder your lines are slanted," and told me I should keep my paper straight.

I tried that for a while, but it was very uncomfortable for me to write with the paper at that angle. So, I turned it back to the 40-degree angle I had it at before, and just made sure the lines were vertical on the paper, not slanted to her when she looked at them. I don't know if she ever noticed that I still turned my paper to write for the rest of the year, but as long as my letters were the way she liked, she seemed happy with my writing, and I could continue to write comfortably.

Sometimes, I think I live life at a 40-degree angle. Sometimes, people try to correct me, but eventually give up. As long as I look vertical to them, they seem happy.

The Fair

Before I was old enough to go to school, I remember going to work with my mother and grandmother at the fair. My grandmother ran the exhibits at the Woman's building: canning, quilting, party decorations, en so fort. People often called her Boss Lady.

There are lots of people I remember from the fair. There was a guard at the Woman's building. His name was Mr. McGee. My grandmother called him Mr. McGoo, probably to his face, but my mother made sure I called him Mr. McGee.

I remember him because he would always tell me to check the coin return on the pay phone, because people sometimes forgot to get their change. I would find a dime when he told me to check, and once a quarter. I don't remember when I realized that he was putting the coins in the return before he would tell me to check, but I remember how exciting it was to find a dime that someone else had just over looked. Later years, the fair moved from the building at the park to tents in a field. I didn't see Mr. McGee anymore, but I will always remember him. He was a kind man.

I was older when the fair was in the tents, and I would get to go with Mother to work on weekends and before school started. Cool, crisp mornings, flannel shirts, and the smell of wood chips on the ground. They would prepare the exhibits days before the fair opened, dress the tables with paper skirts, hang the quilts, make sure everything was displayed nicely for the judges. And make sure all the ribbon winning entries were displayed nicely after the judges had been there.

The quilting ladies were never satisfied with the display; Ethel's was covering up too much of Agnes's, which was hanging over the best corner of Ruth's. My grandmother mostly ignored them. She would just say things like, "they bring the same quilts every year; her grandmother made that one. We've seen enough of it already."

Mr. and Mrs. Lamb were in charge of the photography exhibit. They owned a camera store in town. There were no digital cameras, no instagram, no facebook, no selfies or pics of peoples lunch. Each photograph was a work of art. They would tell me about each slide and photograph, and ask me which I liked. It made me feel very grown up. They were the type of adults, like my grandmother, who talk to children like they talk to adults, like they remember being kids. I think of them when I sell my photography at festivals now.

I remember the people who worked at the games at the fair too. My grandmother would take me around to play the carnival games, and we would always win. I suspect now that the carnies let the Boss Lady's grandson win any of the games that could be rigged. And I know that she would spend enough quarters to make sure I won the ones that were just a game of odds. But at the time, I was certain we were the luckiest two people at the fair.

I think the most important memories are of how my grandmother treated people at the fair. She had to deal with everyone, from the white society garden club women that entered their prize roses in the flower show, to the poor black women that worked as the cleaning crew. I would say Granny treated everyone the same, but that's not true; She had much more respect for the cleaning women than she did the society wives.

For some perspective, these memories are from a time not long after people sat down at the counter at Woolworth's, and were arrested for peacefully demanding to be served, and my grandmother was born in 1900, and used words that people born in 1900 would use. Today she would sound like a bigot, or a rapper, but her words were only words, and were far out weighed by her actions.

I remember one of the cleaning ladies was looking for my grandmother. The cleaning ladies did not call my grandmother Boss Lady; they called her Granny, like many family friends did. When she asked one of the Garden Club ladies if she had seen Granny, the lady said no as if it were an insult to ask. When Granny walked in, and the woman said, "oh there she is," the society woman was quite confused as to how my grandmother could be the woman's granny. My grandmother and the cleaning woman shared a laugh about it after the Garden Club woman left.

After the fair was over, and the tents were being cleaned out, my grandmother would save the left behind canned foods for the cleaning crew. I did not see a white woman giving food to some black women. In a time when upper society was still blatantly fighting equality, I saw a hard working woman who had come through the great depression, making sure other poor hard working women got what help she could give them. I saw a respect between people. I don't think the whole race difference even occurred to me then. It was not until later in life, looking back at what I had learned from my grandmother, that I realized, in a time when the problems of racial equality in our country had barely begun to be addressed, I had seen a camaraderie that transcended race, and I had been taught that people are not all equal, but it is not race or gender that separates us, it's our actions, and how we treat those around us.

Do Unto Others

My mother and I were riding down the road, just about to pass Ed's Groceries. Ed was the local grocer that always gave us each a piece of candy as our mother paid for the groceries, but that's another memory. Suddenly, there was a loud crash, a car wreck. I didn't see it happen. My mother pulled over.

I had to wait in the car. I'm not sure how old I was, but I remember thinking that this was unusual that I was to stay in the car alone. And looking back, maybe the reason I didn't see it happen was that I was not tall enough to see out of the car well.

She came back to the car quickly. A woman was hurt. Mother had come back for blankets. We always had blankets in the trunk. I guess it wasn't really a blanket, but a moving mat. I never really knew why, but I still keep one in my car.

I sat in the car waiting, wondering about the woman, wondering why she needed blankets, realizing that my mother had forgotten all about where we were going, and had stopped to help, and had given away our blanket to someone that needed it, someone we didn't even know.

I don't know if I realized then that my parents taught me by actions more than by words. But I knew my mother was doing something good. And at that moment understood that is what we were supposed to do, stop to help, give people what we can, even if we don't know them.

Mother's Strength

One of my earliest memories was the day I realized how strong my mother was. I was riding my tricycle under the big oak tree with the swing. My mother was sitting in a lawn chair with her feet propped up in another. They were those aluminium frame lawn chairs with the nylon straps woven for the seat and back. Suddenly, Mother yelled, "Don't move!" I had no idea what was wrong, but I didn't move. Then I saw it. A big snake was crawling between the lawn chairs, below her legs.

Now, I was just a kid, so my memory of the size of the snake could be distorted. That is if I didn't have the chairs for reference. The snake was longer than the chairs were wide, and it was not stretched out straight either.

I don't recall how my mother got out of the chairs. That may have been an amazing acrobatic feat in and of itself, but I remember that she was out of the chairs, and standing there with a huge rock. There is no childhood distortion of the size of the rocks. The rock is still there in the yard today. It's one of a circle of rocks that was on the property when my parents bought it. It may have been from the foundation of an old house, or it may have been where the Cherokee camped as they rested at the spring near our house on the Trail Of Tears. Regardless of who set it in the circle, my mother had taken it from it's resting place. It was and is a rough, roundish shape rock, with a diameter of a foot and a half or more.

She lifted the rock up high, and thrust it onto the snake. She did not carry the rock waist high, and drop it on the snake. She raised the rock, and from a relatively safe distance, sent it with some force onto the snake's head.

When my dad came home, we we're all excited to show him the snake Mother had killed, the rock still there on top of it. As he rolled rock back to where Mother had got it, I reminded him that Mother had picked the rock up. As an adult, I'm sure my dad could have picked up the rock also; there was no urgency in returning it to the circle, no need to strain back muscles. But it really emphasized to me as a small child, just how strong my mother was, when it was important.

Family Luck

Luck. Are we born with it? Do we make our own? Can you find it? Can you give it away? I would say I inherited being lucky. Maybe I was lucky to get the genes I inherited. My mother had a knack for finding four leaf clovers. Just walking through the yard, she could always look down and say, "here's another one". She would put them in little bottles in the kitchen window.

My grandmother was always finding them, too. Granny would tape them to Susan B Anthony dollars and give them away as good luck pieces. She was lucky at other things, too. For example, Granny was boss lady of the exhibit tents at the fair. The canning, the quilts, the crafts, they were all displayed in the tents that Granny was in charge of. There are lots of memories there, but back to the lucky ones.

There were games at the fair. Put a quarter on a colored dot, and if the ball bounced in the hole for that color, you win a prize. Granny would take me to play the games. We always won. We won at the 'pick up a duck' game, too. Little plastic yellow ducks would float around in a circle, through a tunnel, and for a quarter, you would pick one up as it came out of the tunnel to see what prize you won by the letter on the bottom.

S for small, M for medium, and L for large. When Granny paid, we always won a large.

Now that I'm older, I realize Granny put a quarter on all the colors, so we couldn't loose. Also, I am fairly certain the duck game was rigged, and the large prize ducks were stuck in the tunnel until the man running the game flipped a switch. My grandmother being a boss lady may have helped out with that game; No carnie was going to cheat the Boss Lady's grandson, not out of fear, but mutual respect.

Similarly, my grandmother could always get the prize I wanted from a gum ball machine. I don't know how many quarters she spent to get it, but I always thought how lucky we were to get just the one I wanted.

My sister was doing the same thing for her granddaughter one day. I wondered if my grandniece thought she was lucky too, or if she realized what my sister was doing. Then I thought, you know, she is lucky, and so was I; not everyone is lucky enough to have such a '"Lucky" grandmother.

We were born lucky. Lucky to be born to people who make their own luck, and know how to give it away. Every time I find a four leaf clover, I know it's supposed to bring luck, but it just reminds me how lucky I already am.

Turn Over a Rock

When I was a 8 or 9, I did not know yet why we went to Cherokee every year. I did not put it together that I was told about the trail of tears because of our Cherokee heritage. It was not until I was a teenager that I started to appreciate the history, and not until I was an adult that I started to reconcile the things I had decided were truths as a child with the beliefs of my ancestors.

I grew up in a Church of Christ. There is no governing body to tell you what you have to believe or how you have to worship to hang that sign out front. When I went to a Church of Christ college, I quickly learned my church was quite different than the others. Much more liberal. But still, it had basic Church of Christ beliefs.

Growing up in the Church, I was not taught about the Cherokee Spirit, and the sacredness of the earth. Not with words anyway. I was not taught of Assisi, or the book of Thomas. But before the things I knew were tinted by knowledge, I saw the light in every leaf, I heard the life in every twig, I felt the soul of every stone.

I was swinging beneath the big oak tree on the hill one day. The wind carried a dogwood blossom from the far side of the yard, and it landed at my feet. I don't think I knew the word sacred then, or what it meant, but as I looked at the the dogwood blossom, that is the best word I have now to describe what I suddenly understood about trees, and rocks, and water. They are sacred. They are life. Every thing of the earth and sky and space are all filled with life.

I knew by then not to try to tell my science teacher that rocks were alive. I would just keep that to myself. And it was much later as an adult, when I read the phrase "Split a piece of wood and i am there, lift a rock and you will find me", that I knew I was not the only one.

Money from a Car Window

 was the youngest of three kids. My dad made a respectable living as a machinist. We were not rich, but we were certainly richer than many of my friends' families. I was never in need, and seldom in want. We had a nice house. I had my own room. I had toys to play with. We didn't have a new car, but we had a car. I knew that I would have breakfast, lunch, and dinner. Some of my friends knew that school lunch might be all they had that day. I never had to worry about food, clothing, shelter, or love.

But I remember this one evening, as we all drove home from somewhere, I was listening from the back seat as my parents were talking about needing to buy milk and bread. They could stop at the 'Milk Jug' just up the road, but it

27

wasn't payday yet and they didn't have any money. Now this is before everyone had credit cards, and debit cards, and after the time when you could ask the Ed the store owner to just put it on your account until payday. So, no money; no milk and bread. This was also a time when you could get milk and bread both with less than a dollar. So, my parents really had NO money until payday.

Then, just as my parents were conceding that it would just have to wait, my dad gets all excited, "Did you see that?" Something had flown out of the window of the car in front of us, and he was pretty sure it was money. Now if anyone could spot money flying from the window of a car going 50 miles an hour, it would be my dad. Actually, not only did he spot the money in flight, he turned around, went back, stopped the car, and found a dollar bill in the weeds on the side of the road in the dusky light.

Now like I said before, I never had to worry about food, clothing, or shelter. It was not that we would all go to bed hungry if we didn't get the milk and bread that evening. It would just have been convenient if we could get the milk and bread now, while we were already near a store, and if we didn't have to wait until payday and the check could be cashed.

So it was no miraculous feeding of the multitude with 40 loaves and fishes, but it was a moment that I will always remember. An incident that still reverberates in my thoughts

whenever I start to think, "how will I ever pay off this credit card?" or "What if this job ends in August?" Whenever those kinds of worry start clogging up the synapses, I think, "pennies from heaven, dollars from car windows, consider the lilies of the fields, and remember the dollar in the weeds."

Quiet Time

First grade. Quiet time. We had to put our heads down in our arms on our desks. And be quiet and still. We sat with 4 kids to a table. The boy across from me had a small store bought toy he was playing with. I began to pretend I had something also. Not to make him think I did, but just to amuse myself. I was quite imaginative.

The boy across from me whispered, "you don't have anything." We were not supposed to talk, so I didn't answer. And continued my make believe. He repeated his taunt. Then Joey, the boy next to me, handed me a ball. A rather large metal ball. About an inch in diameter. As much as I enjoyed imagining, I was in awe of this wondrous new toy. I had never seen such a thing. The boy across from me made some remark that it was not a real toy. I just thought how much more interesting the metal ball was than his toy, and ignored him.

After quiet time was over, I told Joey thanks and handed him the ball. He told me it was a ball bearing, and his dad had given it to him, and he could get more.

He let me keep it.

I still have it. It used to sit on a shelf, sometimes in a wooden box on my dresser, sometimes in storage, but always there somewhere. And always here in my memory. And when I see it, or think of it, I remember Joey. I forget the other kid's name, but I remember Joey, and an act of kindness and generosity, and I am reminded there are lots of wondrous things in the world, waiting to amaze us. Simple, wonder full things.

99 cent Space Program

One of my fondest memories of my grandmother is the time she ordered a model lunar lander for me. I had watched the moon landing on TV, and wanted to be an astronaut. School was out at the time, but the schools sent the buses to pick up all the kids, and take them to school so they could watch the moon landing on TV. I thought it was great that we made an event out of it. We had a TV, but most of the kids in my class, or my school for that matter, probably did not. So, while at the time I didn't appreciate how caring the teachers were that arranged the event, I now see it for the true spirit of teaching that it was.

The kids in my class went into Miss Owens room to watch the landing. I'm not sure everyone in the room cared about how amazing it was that we had landed on the moon. I think some kids just saw it like a movie. I on the other hand was totally convinced that one day I would be going to the moon myself.

I found an ad in a magazine for a model lunar lander, just like the real one. I couldn't read all of the ad, but I could read "Lunar Lander", "Free!", "Just 99cents". My grandmother, who is one of the people who taught me to believe I can be anything in life that I want, was easy to convince that a future astronaut should certainly have a

free for 99 cents model lunar lander. So, she sent in the 99 cents, and 2 to 3 weeks later I received my very own lunar lander. It came in separate white plastic pieces, and once assembled, it was about 3 inches tall. It was the most wonderful toy I had ever owned.

Now, the catch was, in all that small print that I could not read, it said that the model lunar lander was free (99 cents for postage), but that I was now also signed up for a new educational toy every month for a year, for only $1.99 a month (plus postage). At this time, $1.99 could buy 10 gallons of gas or more. My mother now had to pay that each month for the next year. Fortunately, my mother is another one of the people who taught me to believe I can be anything in life that I want. And who also taught me to read the fine print, and think for myself. The wise words, "Is that what someone told you?" was all she had to say to let me know I might want to look a little deeper into a thing before I believed it.

I received some other great toys that year. Some were toys like children played with in other countries or cultures. It was indeed an educational program, and it was something I enjoyed. But after that first $1.99 toy arrived, with the bill, "free for 99 cents" became one of those phrases my mother and I would say as a joke; anytime something sounded to good to be true, we would say, "it's free for 99 cents."

Coffins

My brother-in-law's brother died this week. He is to be cremated. Neither my brother-in-law or I know exactly how we feel about that. One of my sisters wants to be cremated also. I suppose, if the ashes are scattered, that it seems natural. Returning the body to the earth, the dust, the universe. Maybe better than being in an airtight coffin.

I remember the first time I saw a coffin. I was two. My grandfather had died. My family is big on open caskets, viewing the dead. I avoid the coffin room. But they had my aunt Rena propped up in hers so you could see her from the next room. Somewhat disturbing to me.

I probably feel that way because of my grandfather's funeral. Now I am told, I was not at the funeral. That I was left with my Mother's family. But when I was an adult, I walked around the same funeral home with Aunt Mae at another funeral, and we recollected about the day, and she confirmed my memories.

At my grandfather's funeral, someone at the funeral home, I think it was his business partner, Elmer, lifted me up so I could see my grandfather. I should say, my grandfather's body. Even at two, I did not associate the thing in the coffin with the man who had taught me how to fold toast into triangles instead of rectangles.

Another memory I am told is incorrect, but I remember where everyone was sitting at my grandmother's kitchen table. Me on the right, My dad in the centre, and my grandfather at the end. Maybe it was my Dad that helped me fold it, but it was my grandfather who said, "fold it into a triangle; that's how I eat my toast." Maybe my Dad didn't hear him, or know he was there because he thought he was in the coffin.

But back to coffins. I have never since then cared much for coffins, especially opened ones. I'm not sure how I feel about my body being put into one. I do feel like I want my body to return to the earth, as my spirit will return to the universe. It seems right. But then, that corpse I leave behind will be for others to do with as they feel right. I will not care.

I do have one good memory related to coffins. I went with my Grandmother to pick hers out. She had everything pre-arranged once the life insurance company sent her a check because she had outlived the terms of the insurance. She died at 97. I helped carry her coffin from the chapel, and to the graveside. And I have now carried my share of them to the grave.

She was one of the great people in my life, and as sad as the day was, I had to smile when I remembered when she picked out the casket I was carrying.

When I first learned that I was to take her to the funeral home to pick out a casket, I admit I was not thrilled. But in her usual way, she made it humorous and fun. She filled out info for her obituary. Made sure it was legal to list the

adopted great grand children as her own. She wouldn't want to do anything illegal after all. Discussed her favorite hymns. And commented on all the different caskets in the casket showroom. If you didn't know, I did not until I saw one, they do have casket showrooms. Just like car showrooms. Check out what's under the hood. The upholstery. See the different paint options.

She was very careful to pick the right one. Nothing too fancy. Nothing to feminine or girly. She felt the padding and the pillows. That one's too firm. That one's too itchy. I swear she was going to climb up into one to try it out. Had the funeral director not been watching, I am certain she would have. We had a good time that day, I think sharing that experience with her made the casket a little lighter to carry. I still avoid looking at open caskets, but how many people can say one of their fondest memories is the day they spent with their grandmother, picking out a coffin.

TV and Nightmares

The first nightmare I remember, I was very young, probably around 2 or 3. I was in the hospital because of an infection in my hand where I had gotten a splinter of some kind in it. At least that is my understanding. I don't remember myself why exactly I was there. But I do remember there were two beds, mine and another boy's. And both of our mothers had a chair beside the beds. That night I had a dream. It is as clear in my mind today as it was then. It was a monkey. There was no setting, no background, just a monkey, as if appearing from the darkness.

It was not an evil monkey, not one from the Wizard of Oz, though I have suspected that they may have been the root of the dream. It was not a particularly scary monkey. It was not jumping or making noise. It was just a monkey. Actually a chimpanzee, but to me then, it was a just monkey.

My reaction to this dream, was to scream aloud. I know it was aloud because the nurses came running into the room. They thought my mother had screamed. For some reason, I thought it was best to let them think that. So, though I was now awake, I pretended to be asleep. I listened as they talked about how I must have had a nightmare. A Nightmare. A dream that scares you. That's what that means. Yes, I think it was a nightmare. Though even then I was not sure WHY it had scared me; it was just a monkey.

Perhaps it was the Wizard of Oz that made me scream at the site of a monkey. TV was the source of nightmares for me. I'm from that TV generation that started with black and white, but soon saw living color. We saw Lucy and Ricky's twin beds become double beds, situation comedies become situation comedies that addressed real social issues, and we saw news shows go from daily events to daily reports on the number of dead in Vietnam.

One of my first memories of TV is my mother listening to the radio in the kitchen, and something the announcer said made her stop what she was doing, and we went to the living room to turn on the television. I was sitting in the living room floor as I tried to see what she had to watch so urgently. The president had been shot. I didn't know who he was, but I knew he must have been very important to everyone, because it was on the TV, and my mother was very sad and upset. I asked her questions about him, and she explained, but mostly we listened and watch, and the man on TV told what had happened. Before this TV was cartoons to me. Now this box had a more serious purpose.

Later, after I had a better understanding of death, The TV again brought serious information. The draft, the death toll, the protests, the war. My sisters friends were approaching draft age, I heard them talk about it. I watched intently as the TV showed the dead. At 6 years old, I thought I would have to go to war when I turned 18, and that I would die. I had decided at that age, I would not kill. If they sent me to the front lines, I would be shot rather than shoot; because since I was going to die, I would not have my last action in my life be to kill another. At age 6, I was resigned that this was my fate.

The images I saw on TV, and the things of war I heard family and friends talking about, were a source of nightmares. I never told anyone about the nightmares, or my decision to be killed rather than kill. Like the Monkey Dream, I decided to keep those things to myself. To this day, I really don't know why I did that. You could say a six year old had been taught somehow not to talk about being scared, but I was far too young when I had the Monkey Dream for it to have been environment. I think the personality trait of not discussing dreams and ideas must have been in my genetics from the beginning.

One bad result of my reluctance to disclose my nightmares was that my mother assumed it was monster shows on TV that caused them. Therefore, I was not allowed to watch more than one monster show a day. Now by monster shows, I mean the Munsters, the Adams Family, and Dark Shadows. My sister tried to persuade my mother that the Munsters and Adams Family were by no means a source for nightmares. She was always supporting me, and after all, if I could not watch two monster show, neither could she. But the rule stayed, because I never told anyone that the nightmares were not about frankensteins or vampires, but about real monsters like the war I had seen on the news.

Dana

All my life, I have kept things to myself: my dreams, my nightmares, my fears, my hopes. When I started second grade, I was bussed to a different school. I cried and pleaded to be able to go to the old school. I was so distraught that my mother took me to the old school on the first day. There were lists on each door with the names of the students in each class. We went to all the second grade doors just trying to find a way to show me I had to go to the other school, or maybe a little bit of her was hoping my name would have accidentally been left on one of the lists. Because she knew my heart was breaking. I didn't tell her why, maybe she knew that too, but I never told her.

Every decision we make, changes something. It may be minor, or minuscule, with no consequence to the rest of our life. But even the smallest decision may have great impact. If you take a different way home one day, maybe nothing, or maybe you miss the car that ran the stop sign. Or you go the same way, but slow down for a minute to look for something in the car seat, and the car that ran the stop sign misses you. Or I refuse to suck up to the boss, and when layoffs have to be made, I lose my job. I didn't decide to quit, but I made a decision somewhere along the way that may have caused that to happen.

One reason I didn't want to go to the new school was Dana. She was a girl in my first grade class. Most of the time I played alone at recess; I have never been good at meeting people. But sometimes I would play with another kid that had the same name as mine. One day he was picking on Dana while she jumped rope, and she said "I'm going to tell on you, Jimmy". She looked at me and told me "not you, him." She was always nice to me. I had a big crush on her.

I didn't mention much about Dana to my parents. When they would ask about friends at school, I would list Joey and Dana. They thought I was confused when I would call Dana she and Joey he. Probably because they thought Dana was a boys name, and they thought I was saying Joy. I was pretty sure at 6 I knew the difference, and could not understand their confusion.

But when the second grade started, I knew that going to another school meant I would never see Dana again. Not that it would be a long time, or that I might see her somewhere besides school, but I would never see her again. That made me very sad, and that's part of why I cried, but there was more. Even at seven, I understood this thing about any decision changing other things. I knew that my whole future was just altered in some big way. And this time, I had no choice in the decision. Nothing I had done in my short life could have caused this decision. Nothing I could do as a seven year old could undo it. I had no control over what I felt was not a good decision for me.

When I was in 6th grade, I tried to share my loss of Dana and how decisions change our lives with the new girl I had a crush on, let's call her Mary. She was the smartest girl in the school, but she didn't get it. She said I was living in the past. Sang that song "lookin' out my backdoor'" and said that was me. Image one 12 year old telling another 12 year old that they are living in the past. Maybe she's right. Seems time doesn't pass for me like it does for other people; memories of Dana and of Mary are just a moment ago to me. I think perhaps time and space is a little more warped for me than others, as if they are headed in a straight line, and I keep going off on some tangent line to the left only to meet up with them again later.

But I'm not living in the past, I just try to understand it, and use it to make decisions in the future. And sometimes people don't understand my decisions, so I still keep my reasons, my dreams, my beliefs mostly to myself. And have since before the first grade, where I met Dana, and where I learned to draw straight vertical lines, while keeping my paper at 40 degrees to the left.

Selected Poetry

The Milkyway Man

he watched the stars as if they were home,

dreamed of a place where there was no war,

no hatred, no cruelty.

this place surely could not be home.

he was as much of a stranger here

as someone who would come from the stars.

he was born to this place,

but somehow he knew

home was somewhere else

someother time perhaps

or someother reality

but not this place

he watched the stars as if he would go there someday,

a stranger coming home for the first time,

again, finally.

the milkyway dansed through the sky.

his dreams swirled through the stars

like the night swallows that danse around the tower.

they fill the sky each dusk,

and his mind soars with them

to somewhere else

someother time perhaps

or someother reality

but not this place

years and dreams have past

the stars still danse

the swallows still soar

and he still dreams

a little less certain that he'll make it home

but he still dreams

and the milkyway still fills him with wonder

and the birds still bring him peace

and his soul still danses like the swallow

through the stars

to somewhere else

someother time perhaps

or someother reality

but not this place

Over Gothab

somewhere over Gothab

I could feel the icy breath of the wind over the ice

It was a peaceful touch

And I am but me

And I am the multitude

I am but a drop of water

And I am the ocean

And the mist and the dew

Somewhere over Gothab

I closed my eyes and dreamed

Of snow covered mountains

And warm white sand beaches

I am but a grain of sand

I am but a flake of snow

And I am the frozen ice of the poles

And I am the rock and sand

From Alaska to the tip of South America

Somewhere over Gothab I sleep

Turn Over a Rock

When I was a child

Before I knew of the Cherokee Spirit

Before I heard of Assisi

Before I read the phrase

Turn over any rock and I am there

Before the things I knew were tinted by knowledge

I saw the light in every leaf

I heard the life in every twig

I felt the soul of every stone

Now there are those who say the science I gain

denies all I knew but I see no conflict

Each quark, each quasar, each photon,

each immeasurable pog of life

proves the things I knew

Those who never turned over a rock

Do not see the proof there

I think perhaps if God spoke directly to them

They would never admit they heard

Bedtime Story

I will sleep sound tonight

with his voice in my ears

with the salty scent of his breath

surrounding me as peaceful dreams envelop me

only in the forest do I feel as safe as I do here

some speak of the forest as a dark foreboding place

but to me she is filled with life

tiny pieces of sun seeping through the trees

to create patterns of light and shadow

dansing on the hemlocks and the laurel

I am no stranger to her - I am not a visitor there

but a part of a glorious tapestry

as I walk across holy ground

And here

here the endless comfort he speaks

stories of days long forgotten by others

wisdom and songs he teaches

I have heard some say how they feel insignificant in his

presence

dwarfed by his magnificence

but they must not listen to him

for he tells me how each of us

is a significant part of the whole

just as each grain of sand he cast upon the shore

or sweeps out to sea

Cracks In The Sky

The light'ning catches the night like a photograph

suddenly the darkness and shadows have form and depth

but only for an instance

only as long as the light floods through

the cracks in the sky

sometimes there's a light

that breaks through my worries

a frozen instance

that makes the darkness disappear

a chance to see

everything clearly

and I realise

the doubts, the fears

these are just shadows

and the thunder that follows

does not frighten me

for I have seen through

the cracks in the sky

This Compasion
(take away the pain)

I do not give you water because I fear hell

But because your thirst makes my mouth dry

And my lips crack

I do not give you bread because I am supposed to

But because your hunger makes me weak

And my stomach growl

I do not give you my coat to earn my salvation

But because the cold wind on your skin

Makes me shiver

And my bones ache

And those that give to pay their way to heaven

Do not despise them

They practice with the hope of achieving

This compassion

That they think is a gift

But the thirst is never quenched

The stomach never full

And when you have no coat to give

This compassion feels more like a curse

Hearts that break call my name

I can feel their pain

It breaks my heart in two

Eyes that cry look to me

To set their spirits free

It breaks my heart in two

I would take away the pain if I could

Danse the stars again you know I would

But I'm only made of clay

Your Eyes

When I saw your eyes

Pools of onyx

How trite and used my words became

But I am entranced by those depths

And I forget any eloquence of language

And your lips captivate me

I long to trace them with my thumb

And cup you face in my hand

The soft formed features

Your warm skin

Makes me remember

A passion I had almost forgotten

We will not speak

Perhaps a glance, a smile, no more than that

But one day I will paint your memory on canvas

In my dreams

I will remember your lips

And your eyes

Addiction
(As Hard As I Try)

As hard as I try

as hard as I fail

you'd think I'd walk away from you

But time after time

I keep coming back again

trying to believe that it's all true

So here I stand

believing in your lie

thinking it's the only way

a boy like me

survives

Time after time

Dream after dream

when I find they're not quite

what them seem

And fight after fight

Pain After pain

I find the tears

aren't worth the gain

Then you come back

serving up your lie

promising a boy like me

that with you I can survive

And time after time

I keep running back to you

wanting to believe that it's all true

But as hard as I try

As hard as I fail

You'd think I'd turn my back

on you

But I stand here now

believing in your lie

knowing it's the only way

a man like me

survives

I Still Believe

a woman stopped me on the street the other day

and bummed some money so she could eat

as i looked around her i could tell

her whole life was a living hell

and no words of comfort i could find

but then she touched my arm as if to ease my mind

and she said

i still believe there's a light

shining on me in the darkest night

the peace train's running just a little late

but it's gonna' be here

any day so hang on

i told her my life has been pretty easy

i seldom want

i rarely need

but sometime it still feels like there's somethin' missing

maybe someone who i could believe

she touched my face and laughed out loud

then disappeared into the crowd

but i still heard her saying

i still believe there's a light

shining on me in the darkest night

the peace train's running just a little late

but it's gonna' be here

any day so be strong

a good friend called me up yesterday

life's been hard on him

it's taken so much away

he said "maybe this world's already ended

and the saved have already gone

we keep praying for redemption

but maybe we're just on our own"

so i told him

i still believe there's a light

shining on me in the darkest night

the peace train's running just a little late

but it's gonna' be here

any day

Out Of The Water

Out of the water

i stumble through the sands

too afraid to fall

too tired to stand

who will i be

at the end

of the day

when the face

in the mirror

simply fades into grey

flashes of insight

like cracks in the sky

i go searching for answers

finding only alibis

who shall i be

at the end of the day

when the face in the mirror

simply fades into grey

the air i've been breathing

can no longer sustain

the truth i held constant

can no longer remain

i leave with the wind now

to chase across the sky

and danse through the stars

and wear them in my eyes

and who shall i be

at the end of the day

when the face in the mirror

simply fades into grey

Out of the water

i stumble

i stumble

and cross the sands

Thank You

for reading my stories

and letting me share my memories

- J. Smith Kirkland

Printed in Great Britain
by Amazon